# Favorites for Two

Arrangements by Pete Deneff

Disney characters and artwork © Disney
Disney/Pixar elements © Disney/Pixar

*Based on the "Winnie the Pooh" works, by A.A. Milne and E.H. Shepard

ISBN 978-1-70515-361-1

Visit Hal Leonard Online at
**www.halleonard.com**

Contact Us:
**Hal Leonard**
7777 West Bluemound Road
Milwaukee, WI 53213
Email: info@halleonard.com

In Europe contact:
**Hal Leonard Europe Limited**
42 Wigmore Street
Marylebone, London, W1U 2RN
Email: info@halleonardeurope.com

In Australia contact:
**Hal Leonard Australia Pty. Ltd.**
4 Lentara Court
Cheltenham, Victoria, 3192 Australia
Email: info@halleonard.com.au

# THE BALLAD OF THE LONESOME COWBOY
from TOY STORY 4

CELLOS

Music and Lyrics by
RANDY NEWMAN

# BE OUR GUEST
from BEAUTY AND THE BEAST

CELLOS

Music by ALAN MENKEN
Lyrics by HOWARD ASHMAN

**Moderately, in 2**

# BELLE
from BEAUTY AND THE BEAST

CELLOS

Music by ALAN MENKEN
Lyrics by HOWARD ASHMAN

**Spiritedly**

# CRUELLA DE VIL

from 101 DALMATIONS

CELLOS

Words and Music by
MEL LEVEN

# A DREAM IS A WISH YOUR HEART MAKES

from CINDERELLA

CELLOS

Music by MACK DAVID
and AL HOFFMAN
Lyrics by JERRY LIVINGSTON

# FOR THE FIRST TIME IN FOREVER

from FROZEN

CELLOS

Music and Lyrics by KRISTEN ANDERSON-LOPEZ
and ROBERT LOPEZ

# HOW DOES A MOMENT LAST FOREVER

from BEAUTY AND THE BEAST

CELLOS

Music by ALAN MENKEN
Lyrics by TIM RICE

# IN SUMMER
from FROZEN

CELLOS

Music and Lyrics by KRISTEN ANDERSON-LOPEZ
and ROBERT LOPEZ

# INTO THE UNKNOWN

from FROZEN 2

CELLOS

Music and Lyrics by KRISTEN ANDERSON-LOPEZ
and ROBERT LOPEZ

# JUST AROUND THE RIVERBEND
from POCAHONTAS

CELLOS

Music by ALAN MENKEN
Lyrics by STEPHEN SCHWARTZ

# LAVA
from LAVA

CELLOS

Music and Lyrics by
JAMES FORD MURPHY

# LEAD THE WAY
from RAYA AND THE LAST DRAGON

CELLOS

Music and Lyrics by
JHENÉ AIKO

# NEVER TOO LATE
from THE LION KING 2019

CELLOS

Music by ELTON JOHN
Lyrics by TIM RICE

# THE PLACE WHERE LOST THINGS GO

from MARY POPPINS RETURNS

CELLOS

Music by MARC SHAIMAN
Lyrics by SCOTT WITTMAN
and MARC SHAIMAN

**Gently, not slow**

# REFLECTION
from MULAN

CELLOS

Music by MATTHEW WILDER
Lyrics by DAVID ZIPPEL

# REMEMBER ME
## (Ernesto de la Cruz)
### from COCO

CELLOS

Music and Lyrics by KRISTEN ANDERSON-LOPEZ
and ROBERT LOPEZ

**Moderately fast**

# SPEECHLESS

from ALADDIN

CELLOS

Music by ALAN MENKEN
Lyrics by BENJ PASEK
and JUSTIN PAUL

# THAT'S HOW YOU KNOW
from ENCHANTED

CELLOS

Music by ALAN MENKEN
Lyrics by STEPHEN SCHWARTZ

# TOUCH THE SKY
from BRAVE

CELLOS

Music by ALEXANDER L. MANDEL
Lyrics by ALEXANDER L. MANDEL
and MARK ANDREWS

# TRY EVERYTHING

from ZOOTOPIA

CELLOS

Words and Music by SIA FURLER,
TOR ERIK HERMANSEN and MIKKEL ERIKSEN

# UNDER THE SEA

from THE LITTLE MERMAID

CELLOS

Music by ALAN MENKEN
Lyrics by HOWARD ASHMAN

# WINNIE THE POOH

from THE MANY ADVENTURES OF WINNIE THE POOH

CELLOS

Words and Music by RICHARD M. SHERMAN
and ROBERT B. SHERMAN

# YOU'VE GOT A FRIEND IN ME
from TOY STORY

CELLOS

Music and Lyrics by
RANDY NEWMAN